on/*me*

Caitlin Press Inc.

8100 Alderwood Road,
Halfmoon Bay, BC V0N 1Y1
www.caitlin-press.com

Cover design by Vici Johnstone
Text design by Monica Miller
Cover art by Francine Cunningham
Printed in Canada

Caitlin Press Inc. acknowledges financial support from the Government of Canada and the Canada Council for the Arts, and the province of British Columbia through the British Columbia Arts Council and the Book Publisher's Tax Credit.

Library and Archives Canada Cataloguing in Publication

Cunningham, Francine, 1984- author.
    On/me / Francine Cunningham.
Poems.
ISBN 9781773860169 (softcover)

Canadiana 20190116501 |

LCC PS8605.U52 O5 2019 | DDC C811/.6—dc23

on/*me*

by

Francine Cunningham

CAITLIN PRESS

Dedicated to my family

CONTENTS

On How to Keep on Living
/ *Passing*

i move through the world passing—

as mentally well
as a white woman
as over my grief
as successful

i am none of these things,
at least not fully

On Identity
/ Origin of a Designation

i hadn't heard the term *white passing* until recently
it wasn't something i grew up with—*white passing,*
said like bad words, strung together to hurt, to designate, to demarcate

like i should be something other than white
like i should have skin other than what i have
like i was called *white buffalo* growing up, a difference in the lineup of cousins

marked but not known why

mixed blood
métis
half-breed
hybrid
off reserve
scottish
indian
steinhauer
a part of the land
aboriginal
cunningham
quantifiable
belgian
a bill c
indigenous
cree
calahasian
urban
non-speaker
prairie dweller
native
status card holder

the buck stops with me,
my mom always said that to my sisters and me growing up

the buck stops with me,
as if to say
you are not indian in the government's eyes
you are not indian in the people's eyes
you are not
indian

but then why do i hear cree in my dreams?

On Mental Illness
/ Lists

Francine:

general anxiety disorder
possible borderline personality disorder
bipolar ii disorder
depression
ptsd

family (a combination or singular):

general anxiety disorder
borderline personality disorder
bipolar disorder
multiple personality disorder
schizophrenia
paranoid schizophrenia
ptsd
attempted suicide
suicide
addiction (alcoholism, drug abuse, gambling)

On Tradition
/ *Camping*

sometimes i get jealous when i listen to other people's stories
    of their traditional upbringing, but then i think, they never had kfc
to hear some of my contemporaries tell it
they were raised on bush meat, fresh air and wild springs
they lived all traditional
i lived in the city
we went camping
in the driveway of my grandparents' trailer park,
in the camper they drove when they sold at powwows

On Love
/ Love Letter I

loving you is like hearing music in my dreams
elusive,
tantalizing,
forever echoing in the farthest reaches of my consciousness
rising to the surface
for a brief moment
clear and piercing,
drowning out all other sounds

On Family
/ Mother

met my father in a horse stall
kept dating him even after
their first date
when he took her to a restaurant
and dined and dashed

i never understood why
she chose him
when they were so unalike

married twenty years
still don't know if either of them was happy

locked herself in her room for
almost a year when he finally left
sitting in the living room with my sisters
listening to the sound of her rocking chair
thump against the floor of her bedroom

learned to take care of myself
when i learned my parents
wouldn't
or couldn't
or maybe they were just human
and going through
the complicated motions of life

On Teasing
/ Aunties

head thrown back in laughter,
hands out whacking shoulders

On Mental Illness
/ Fault Lines

i've never known what my faults were
only that they existed,
decided long before i was born

the faults lay in lines
carved into skin
the unseen codes
the mess
of who i am

under the surface
unseen
until they rip and groan
the two halves
in a violent thrust
making waves as tall as tsunamis
cracking ground
uprooting trees
creating new vistas

in the memory of my cells
trauma
passed down from generation
                        to generation
                                to generation
residential schools
indian sanatoriums
sexual abuse
mental illness
alcoholism
addiction

each of these lay heavy
across who i am
some more recent than others

all surfacing
creating upheaval
twisting through the landscape of who i am
who i might one day be

waiting for the earthquake
is sometimes worse than the
earthquake itself
the anticipation of destruction
of needing to rebuild
of knowing what work lies ahead
but understanding
that for every good day there will be many more bad ones

knowing that these fault lines were formed in the womb
that i had no choice over them
is comforting
sometimes
other times the rage and fear consume me
because what can i do?
you can't patch the mantel
you can only prepare
for the rupture,
for what happens after

learn to stand in doorways
to avoid falling wires

On Identity
/ Descriptions of Self from Outside of Self

indianhalfbreednativefirstnationsaboriginalindigenousmétiscreendn
treaty6urbancityoffreserveeducatedyoungpersonbeaderwriterartist
whiteskinbrownhairgreeneyesoneofthegoodonesseperatedstatusmooch
prairieheaddresswearingspiritualwarriorrecoveredsavageteepeeliving
freeloaderluckysurivorredskinanimaltotemlovingculturetraditional
pancakebuttbannockmakingwomanofthekitchenrenegadeforward
movinghorseridernobellovinglonghairedsquawdreamcatchingearth
lovingteacherlisteningtothewindonthebackofhistoryconquered
vanquishedkilledthrivingalivestillbloodnationhooddancingtraitors
identityoutsideofselfinsideofself

On TV
/ Pocahontas

going to my granny and grandpa's
so proud to show them
other natives on tv
they were sad

On Love
/ Love Letter II

i never thought you
until i did,
and now i can't think anything else

On Tradition
/ Doorways

hide hung in doorways,
deer, maybe moose
door not needed when the skin of an animal will do

this cabin built by hands
that now lay under thick blankets in the heat of the afternoon

i am sitting in the corner
a little stool under me
his words drift in and out
cree flowing from me to him, him to me
young enough to have the words enter my cells
become trapped
sneak out in the dreams
of the adult me

On Mental Illness
/ Bipolarism on the Axis

this disease rips you apart
it breaks your heart
it throws you to chaos

this disease is the eater of dreams
of life that could be lived
it locks you away in your bedroom
cuts open your skin
causes lightning in your brain
steals sleep,
dreams

this disease takes you to the places where people walk alone

it brings you to the highs of glory,
of life lived to the fullest,
energy and brilliance and greatness
it shoves you into the blinding heat of the sun
until you scream for more pain because
you can handle anything—and then what's over there?

a speeding dart of darkness hits you in the chest
and everything tumbles
and you are nothing
and worthless
and why are you even alive

this disease feels hopeless
living on this balancing beam feels hopeless
and you're exhausted from trying to smile
from saying everything's fine
from hiding the worst of it
you're exhausted from living
and so you scream into your pillow in the middle of a sun-drenched afternoon

you plead on hands and knees to god, to the creator,
   to anybody who might be listening

but this disease, it is you
and you know only it
and maybe that can be comforting too

On Purpose
/ When Not Writing I

hollow echoes in my
empty chest
filled with half-formed thoughts
laughter stuck,
rotten in my throat
tears drift in automatic responses
but still, that hollow
that cavernous
place

On Mental Illness
/ *Nothing of Worth*

to measure a life,
the worth of it at least,
is futile

but for me,
i haven't measured up
i don't think

i feel it inside of me,
this wastefulness of breath

perhaps if i knew the reason,
the *why* of why i am alive,
i would be able to better match my efforts to the plan of it
but i am bereft of reason, of purpose

to be loved, perhaps
to love
neither of which i have done
neither of which i have felt the stirring to do
the emptiness inside of me marking me a freak

and what if i do love
and we fight,
are at odds every day,
but still claim love?

have a child,
maybe two,
would that make this life one that has worth?

and what of the past?
all this time spent idle?

if i were to publish the greatest story ever told,
would my life *mean* something then?

or would it just be something that i *did*?
like everything else i've *accomplished*

what would it look like,
feel like—
to know i didn't waste my life?

On Food
/ Bannock

baked, square or round globes formed from the rims of used pickle jars
i don't have milk, use water
i don't have eggs, that's okay, only some people use them anyways
i only have a bit of sugar, that's okay, throw it in
don't knead it too much or you'll have flat bannock bums
jam vs honey vs peanut butter vs butter vs melted cheese vs fully loaded

On Family
/ Grandmother

taken
can her story really be told without that word?

taken off reserve
away from her family
away from her land
away from her language
away from everything she knew

taken
her hair
her innocence
her self

taken
to a new life
in a city that settled her
in a settler city
in a new home
with new family members

taken to an indian sanatorium one winter night
met an indian man
who took her into his heart
and who she took into hers

taken
with nine children,
grandchildren
great-grandchildren
great-great-grandchildren

taken into history
but it started off
by being taken

On Identity
/ Maybe It's More Than the Lights and Pixels

watching the cowboys and indians on tv i realized that i could play both roles
my left half would try and kill my right half
my right half would out-survive my left half
the two halves would ride around and around in circles
trying to catch each other

On Love
/ Love Letter III

i am learning a song on the ukulele for you
i know
i'm cute

On Mental Illness
/ *Addiction*

every day starts with good intentions
  no, *great* intentions
    every *great* day lasts until the afternoon
    every *great* night is failure

i'll start again tomorrow

    it'll be a *great* day!

On Grief
/ Hospital Visits

my mother never had a chance to be white passing
she was always known by the brown in her skin,
the cree in her features,
what strangers thought she was,
never known for the unseen qualities, the details
her faith, her garden lush in summer, her laughter that burst through spaces
what was seen was beyond her control
people's perceptions
what they thought they knew

when i was a teenager we moved to a small town in the north
it was during the oka crisis
protests strung along the country
my mom, scared to go outside
 these people will think i'm one of them, the bad indians,
 the protesting indians
she was afraid, see,
of getting insults hurled at her, beaten up
in a new place with faces that didn't know her details
that only knew the colour of her skin

when she got sick, really really sick,
she went to the hospital
and they didn't see the details then either
so used to "fixing up" the problem brown people
they didn't see the real her
so they sent her away
and so she came back
again
and again
and again
and they always sent her away
pneumonia
that's what they called her lung cancer until she couldn't breathe anymore

until it was stage iv and in her back and brain
because by then they couldn't deny her anymore
they couldn't see her as a drunk indian, someone to be forgotten
because they knew then
it was the tumour in her brain, not her skin colour,
that was the problem
but even then, when they knew,
they wouldn't give her morphine for the pain
still convinced she was her skin colour and their perception
she had to fight for relief
she had to fight for them to see the details
never mind my mom never drank,
didn't smoke, didn't do drugs, hardly ever swore, was a christian
none of those details mattered
and after the first stirrings of pain in her chest twelve months before
she was gone

On Family

/ Sisters

the langoliers
peeling pink frozen popcorn off the bottom of the freezer
ringette
barbies
the stand
the green la-z-boy in the living room that was perfect for reading
hand-me-down dresses
car rides
singing along to
    the mamas and the papas, don mclean, queen, eric clapton, acdc,
    hank williams, johnny cash
afternoons spent sprawled in silence with our books
fighting so hard you throw a ham at the other's head
making movies in the backyard
dying each other's hair in the bathtub
confessions in the dark
holding hands during the birth of babies
seeing the northern lights and still not being convinced it wasn't an alien invasion
tattoos
endless canasta around a dining room table
laughing so hard you can't breathe

On Love
/ Unrequited Love (The Safest Kind of Love)

love,
sitting on the tip of my tongue
slipping into the silence between words
don't say it, don't say it
my inner monologue against the tensing of muscles
holding in this secret

love,
one sided
coming up against your wall

On Mental Illness
/ Depression

the only time i felt good today was when i went back to bed
but it was a fake feeling good
because going back to bed will only make me feel better for a little while
i'll feel worse later,
i always feel worse later

On Teasing
/ Love

if i've never teased you
i don't love you

On Living
/ Burning

i sometimes think about the fact that
if i had been born in another time
or even a different place
i could have been burned
or stoned to death
sterilized against my knowledge
committed to an asylum
traded
not my own person

all because i am a woman

i read
i went to school
i want things for myself
i believe i should be able to speak and be listened to
i don't think i need a husband and kids to live a good life

i have not been burned or stoned to death
i have control of my reproduction
i am not considered hysterical, crazy or a witch
i am my own person

things could be better but sometimes it's nice to think about the good, too

On Grief
/ Build Up

when i took apart the shower head
i found the body of a beetle
its small legs were stuck in the gaps of the mesh
the body slick, covered in brown slime

i thought of the shower i had taken that morning
the feel of the water as it lapped at my toes
as the drain, clogged with hair, let the water fill up

i thought of the sigh of pleasure i let out
as the heat let me forget, for a moment,
the rusty brown dirt
the box that held you
the darkness of that hole

i pried the body out with a pair of tweezers
hovered over the toilet bowl
but felt sadness

lying on the linoleum
among the cobwebs of stray hair and dust
the disappearing body of the beetle beside me
i thought of you again
without the heat of the shower
without the urge to forget
i thought of you
your disappearing body
and felt my grief

On Identity
/ Ancestral Power

it's hard to feel power from my ancestors when i don't know
who they are,
where they come from,
what their stories are

we share blood
blood shares memory
but i want us to share so much more

my breath over the phone line
but who did they come *from*?
what are their stories?
i don't know, my girl

nighttime thought: what if my ancestors, or at least a few of them, were dicks?
worth derived from knowing where and who you come from
but would it really matter if i did know
because at this point all my knowing would be contained to names
lying dead on pieces of paper

does anyone truly know their ancestors anymore?
did they ever?

do these thoughts make me a bad ndn?

On Mental Illness
/ *Choices*

it is when this black mood comes upon me that i know
life has no meaning
    nothing matters
    nothing is real
    nothing exists

how do i face another day, another hour, another moment knowing
you choose life every moment of your waking life
until you don't

On Tradition
/ Language

kîkwây, my girl
âstam, now
wah wah, you silly girl
namoya, êhê, awas

but i always knew there was more
i listened to it being spoken around the table
a secret language i was supposed to be a part of

On Love
/ Shells

i whispered my love for you
into a shell
threw it into the ocean
for the mermaids to hear
telling my secrets to those
who still believe in love
hoping they will help you see me

On Food
/ Dessert

berries frozen over winter
thawing on the counter until they can be
bathed in creme

On Identity
/ Silence

i.

maybe it's like this for all half-breeds
for all of us in-between
the expectation of who we are
and what we're supposed to be

ii.

a relative i've never met before:
you're so fair,
his eyes roving over my skin
you're so fair,
he repeats in bewilderment,
his fingertips trace the veins in my skin
    like fingertips trace the borders on a map

my skin is lighter than his
fair,
not brown

his eyes dart from my grandmother's face to mine,
searching for the resemblance in shades

you're so fair,
he whispers again

iii.

life lived in a city
not a tipi

life lived with white friends
in a white neighbourhood
passing as white
until i got home

iv.

sitting with my sisters in the hospital
waiting for our mom's brain surgery to be over
for her to live

another native family sharing the space
waiting
on life

security burst through the doors
yelling at the brown faces
across from us
screaming about stolen equipment
demanding to look through bags,
under clothing

that family, just waiting for life
like us

our family left alone
not brown enough
to be disturbed

v.

sitting in the awkward silence
of deciding whether or not to point out that what a colleague said was
incredibly racist
said to my face as if i am a co-conspirator
because my skin colour matches theirs

*those useless natives, they don't pay any goddamn taxes, they should go back and
live in tipis if they want their land back so much*

deciding if getting up and walking away is enough

deciding if fighting is enough

deciding if educating is probable

knowing that i will forever live here
in this space
of in-between

On Purpose
/ When Not Writing II

ink on the rubber stamp
repeatedly pushed against crisp paper
never filled
and so the impression,
more like a ghost
than before

On Death
/ Nîpîy

water pours from the tap
and i'm sad
because i know this won't last forever
there will be a moment in the future when
i remember this free-flowing water
so easy
too easy
and i will remember the waste
and cry

but i am also happy
because there will be a day when i won't
be drinking water that's traumatized

we hold in our cells the memories of the water we drink

what memories are we giving it?

On Mental Illness
/ klo-NAY-zeh-pam

pink, with a soft white centre
numbers engraved on the backside
twice a day, shaken from an orange container
bathed in cool water
on the way down

a pill to quiet the chaos
which lurks
beneath the blanket of chemicals
waiting for release

it will wait
until the pills are gone
then
the shaking will return
fire that races across my back
choking fear

it will wait

fear of death
fear of life

it will wait

pink, with a soft white centre
numbers engraved on the backside
twice a day, shaken with trembling fingers from the orange container

On Identity
/ *Boxed, or Every Form I Fill Out Ever*

please check the following box that defines you best.

are you:

☐ status

☐ non-status

☐ métis

☐ inuit

do i really fit into such a small box?

On Family
/ *Grandfather*

a lasso made from his oxygen tube
thrown over our heads as we whizzed by
racing from the back of the trailer
through the cramped hallway
to the living room
where he sat in his chair
watching us as we played

not knowing him
or at least the details of him
until after he died
the army
the shot to the lung
the tb
the indian sanatorium
the drinking
the smoking
the raising of his girl

i knew the dentures snuck under my dinner plate to scare me
the money slipped into the hands
    of everyone who visited to help pay for gas, groceries
the twiddling of the thumbs over the steering wheel
    while we waited for my grandma
the clock over the door with the man and woman who told us the weather
the radio dialled into classic country
wrestling on the tv
the prick of the finger to check blood sugar
the man who helped bathe my dreams in cree

On Food
/ KFC

the official food of a calahasian feast
skin dripping with oil
fries drowning in gravy
reminiscing about deep-fried corn fritters

On Love
/ Star Matter

in the void between voids
in that blackest of darkness
of not even night
in that permanent cold
that place without breath
we float

between the stars
and their fiery belching heat
we strain to reach
for cold hands to hold in our own

shouting as we pass through
the field of silent boulders
suspended as if arranged in a chess match
by those we cannot fathom
yearning to hear
from the others' lips
the familiar words
i love you

between the matter of stars
we spin and twist, hoping
to catch a glimpse of
the others' face

but we cannot push
against nothing

On Tradition
/ Wishes

there are languages i wish i could speak:

the language of the forest
how to move, how to be still
how to eat, how to survive

the language of love
how to commit, how to be vulnerable

the language of understanding
how to not judge, how to accept faults

the languages of the people i come from
cree
flemish
dutch
german
french
celtic

there are languages i wish i didn't speak:

the language of trauma
how to hide, how to forget until you can't anymore

the language of abuse
how to take it, voice silenced

the language of the government
bill c-31, blood quantum, identifiable, traceable

the language of goodbye
taken in every way

On Mental Illness
/ Slice and Dice

i know you
you are all the feelings that i have,
released through this blade and into my skin
the very best of everything i have
the secret that i crave

On Identity
/ *Blood*

looking through records
tracing my father's blood
half-breeds
strung along the family tree

lesser slave lake
red river
first métis priest in the west

a footnote:
the government of canada is studying the blood of half-breeds in the area
they are known to have a rare blood mutation

a doctor's visit:
i think you may have some sort of blood mutation

i don't bother looking into it
not wanting any more of my family's dna on file
i am alive,
that's all that matters

On Grief
/ *Packing*

cracking egg shells
fertilizer for sunflowers
a simple act that undoes me
leaves me fractured on the kitchen floor
aching,

when we packed up your things,
invaded your closet—
those secret places you kept for yourself
we found bags, multiple,
filled with white-and-brown-speckled shells
each fractured and fragmented
for use in the spring

your garden,
it bloomed this summer
with no help from your shells
kept over winter in the back of my closet

On Family
/ Great Grandparents

love
shown in gestures

rhubarb hung in the rafters
of their cabin over winter
so she could make him
rhubarb pie,
his favourite,
all winter

cree whispered
under blankets
as hands hold on tight
the language of love

rabbits on the trapline
fur for her mittens
moose killed and butchered
for moccasins

gardens dug out every spring
mud hauled from the creek to fill the cracks
between the wood
in the cabin he built for them

love,
shown

sâkihitowin

On Identity
/ Father Apart

in a marriage between a native woman and a white man
the native wasn't the drunk
isn't that funny
no, it isn't,
not really

but i guess my father isn't really a white man
he just looks like it
pale skin, so white you can see the blue veins underneath
clear-blue eyes
red-brown hair
but he has a métis card, the *official* proof
of a family trail

his, our, lineage reads like the story of canada
scotsmen, frenchmen, immigrants working for hudson's bay
forming the west
conquering
marrying native women along the way
having half-breed babies,
    having half-breed babies,
        having half-breed babies,
going through the records,
a cree here
an unknown indian there
someone from an out-east tribe thrown in the middle

my dad once asked me why i identify as being indigenous
as if to say, why did you choose your mom's blood over mine
you're half mine too, he followed up with
just to make sure i knew

but i never knew his parents
i only stepped foot in their apartment once in my life
was shown the plaque on the wall displaying the cunningham family crest

was told of the rolling hills of scotland
as if i really was from there
as if the eyes of my father's parents had ever seen the land
i sat on the plastic-covered couch and wished i could go home
because these people were strangers
lipstick grandma and blue-eyed grandpa,
because they weren't granny and grandpa
the real ones
my mom's parents
the ones i lived with for a time up north
the ones who bathed my dreams in cree as i slept
on the warm floor of their trailer

On Mental Illness
/ General Anxiety Disorder

no no no no no no no no no no no no no no no no no no no no no no no no
stop thinking stop thinking stop thinking stop thinking stop thinki
shut up shut up shut up shut up shut up shut up shut up shut up shu
it's not real it's not real it's not real it's not real it's not real it's not real it's not real it
everything is fine everything is fine everything is fine everything is fine everyt
NO NO NO NO NO NO NO NO NO NO NO NO NO NO NO NO
you're not dying you're not dying you're not dying you're not dying you're no
JUST STOP stop stop stop stop stop stop stop stop stop stop stop sto
1234123412341234123412341234123412341234123412341234123412341234123412
do not go to the emergency room do not go to the emergency room do no
breathe breathe breathe breathe breathe breathe breathe breathe breathe bre
you can do this you can do this you can do this you can do this you can d
no no no no no no no no no no no no no no no no no no no no no no no
stop thinking stop thinking stop thinking stop thinking stop thinking st
shut up shut up shut up shut up shut up shut up shut up shut up shut up sh
it's not real it's not real it's not real it's not real it's not real it's not real it's not real
everything is fine everything is fine everything is fine everything is fine ever
NO NO NO NO NO NO NO NO NO NO NO NO NO NO NO NO N
you're not dying you're not dying you're not dying you're not dying you
JUST STOP stop stop stop stop stop stop stop stop stop stop sto
1234123412341234123412341234123412341234123412341234123412341234123412341
do not go to the emergency room do not go to the emergency room do no
breathe breathe breathe breathe breathe breathe breathe breathe breathe brea
you can do this you can do this you can do this you can do this you can do
no no no no no no no no no no no no no no no no no no no no no no no
stop thinking stop thinking stop thinking stop thinking stop think
shut up shut up shut up shut up shut up shut up shut up shut up shut up shut
it's not real it's not real it's not real it's not real it's not real it's not real it's
everything is fine everything is fine everything is fine everything is fin
NO NO NO NO NO NO NO NO NO NO NO NO NO NO NO NO N
you're not dying you're not dying you're not dying you're not dying you're n
JUST STOP stop stop stop stop stop stop stop stop stop stop sto
1234123412341234123412341234123412341234123412341234123412341234123412
do not go to the emergency room do not go to the emergency room do not go

On Teasing
/ To Make Everyone Laugh

my family:
waaaaahhhhh, just kidding

On Love
/ Full Circle

trace the edge
years worn in our hands
eyes dimmer, but
deeper

fallen in love and out of love
many, many times

but, still—
i am brought back to you

On Questions
/ What If?

the moment a person dies,
it is the exact moment they decide to die,
truly in their soul decide to die
what if there are no accidents?
nothing is random
we choose and then the universe responds with death
what if?

aliens really did influence mankind,
create us?
are our gods?
what if mary was impregnated not by a divine figure,
but instead by an alien race?
what if jesus was their way of teaching us?
all the great prophets,
all the great inventions,
they're behind it all
and they've abandoned us
what if?

nothing is real
what if?

there really are different dimensions?
what if when they turned on the large hadron collider
we went spinning into a mass of fractured time
and that signs really are all around us?
bereinstein vs bereinstain
looney tunes vs loony toons
maybe we can get back
maybe we can't
maybe you're living the life of your dreams in one
maybe you're living your greatest fear in another
what if?

our dreams are reality,
and our waking life is just the place where we collect material for our dreams,
our real lives
what if?

giants really did roam the earth at one time
what if the all the mysterious massive humanoid bones are really theirs?
and what if they really were the offspring
the nephilim,
of angels and men
what if?

time portals really exist,
and people really do slip back in time
just for moments
or hours?
or maybe some unlucky people get stuck
what if?

everything you believed as a child is real?

On TV
/ WWE

if my grandpa was in the living room
wrestling was on

On Grief
/ Fireflies

I don't want her to leave like this.
    Or, I guess I should say *die*.
    That's the true word, right?
    Die.
    I don't want her to die like this. Raving. Spewing hateful words. But I have no choice. And neither does she. The tumours that are eating the healthy flesh in her brain are turning her into someone I don't recognize. They're turning the woman who grew me inside of her, who always made me feel safe, who loved me unconditionally, into a stranger who looks me in the eye and doesn't know who I am.
    But I have no choice. And neither does she.

After she's gone I'm consumed with writing her letters. I stay awake long after my eyes burn, after the voice inside says it's time to sleep, to dream. But I can't sleep until I've written everything I need to say.
    I have to tell her about the boy in the bakery who threw in a free loaf of bread. About the perfect golden light at sunset that I chase every day from different places on the beach. I need to tell her about the house that was consumed in flames and was left smouldering for days, the thick smoke hanging in the air—reminding those of us with houses left standing to hide our emergency money in tinfoil wrapped so tight there is no air for fire to consume. I need to explain to her how beautiful the sparks were, how when they got caught in an updraft they reminded me of fireflies, how I've never seen fireflies and that I don't think that they actually exist, but how can something that beautiful not exist. I need to tell her not to die. But I can't.
    I have no choice. And neither did she.

On Identity
/ *For the Other Mixed-Blood Half-Breed Urban NDNs*

our worth is not derived from where we were not raised
knowing cement streets is not an evil thing
having never set foot on the reserves that our mothers and fathers,
grandmothers and grandfathers came from does not make us less than
having skin that isn't what it's supposed to look like does not make you
unworthy
having memory away from the land does not make you unconnected
not having your ancestral language fill your mouth does not mean you
cannot speak

recognize that no one can take away all that you are
whether you have a little plastic card or not

i work with too many youth who are beaten down, broken
by their own people
by the rest of canada
interhatred
inside hatred
but these youth do not deserve to feel so alone

i grew up feeling in-between
not knowing where i belong
not belonging anywhere
skin unlike my mother's
english instead of cree
scared to go to the land where my people came from
unaccepted
inside and out

tradition, ceremony
words that are spoken cavalierly
for those of us raised away
our tradition is our lived family

On Mental Illness
/ *My Spirit Isn't Happy*

i can feel this truth with every inhalation
i am captured here

i blame the city,
my apartment
the densely packed bodies
i blame the disillusionment of creative energy
i blame social media,
the call of click bait
the negativity that feeds my anxiety
i blame myself

On Death
/ Through Ribs and Things

a boy, with stains of juice ringing his mouth,
turned and asked his mother,
—how long do i have to stay here,
—on earth?

the three of us were gathered
around a glass case
holding the fossil remains of a whale
empty eye sockets staring us down
i watched the mother's face
as she gave me a half smile,
an apology, i think

—i said, how long?
he asked again

the question
it flowed through the bones
drifted up vertebrae
licked its way along the form of played-out life

—i can't wait to go home, this place is dying

there was pain in his voice
as he tried to understand the brown remains under bright lights
he pressed his face against his mirror image
his mother grabbed his arm and pulled him away
my own hand found its way to the glass, pressed against the question

my voice whispered inside the empty voids
where flesh and life used to cling

—how long till any of us make it home?

On Love
/ Still, Beauty

a petal
quietly—it separates, quivers
frail— it drifts, lone
pure—it lands, bruised
motionless, it remains

On Food
/ Fry Bread

the same as baked bannock, but not really
fried up in oil, squares with holes in the middle, round fluffy disks
indian taco base
only for special occasions in my family
same recipe as baked

On Family
/ Father

when he comes home i don't know which man he is going to be
are we going to laugh tonight,
or are we going to cry?
fight?
hide?

am i going to get woken up at midnight
while he walks through the house
howling at the moon?

is he going to come sit on the end of my bed
while i try and fall asleep,
and whisper to me how he wishes he could just die?
that he hates his life and that he is sorry for being a bad parent and that he'll try harder

is he going to make promises he'll never remember?
am i going to spend the evening listening to him tell me the same stories of his life?
am i going to get punished for things i don't understand?

are we going to wrestle on the front lawn with the neighbour's kids while the sun sets?
am i going to have to defend my sisters from his screaming, from the threatened fist?
is he going to pass out early?
will we be left alone?

will he be lighting the front lawn on fire again?
his name written in gasoline, lighting up the neighbourhood

this is the unpredictability of an alcoholic parent

On Mental Illness
/ Calm

seeing but not seeing
earth opening herself up to me

leaving behind my phone, my paper, my ink
entering the forest as myself
taking off shoes
walking with needles underfoot
sitting beside a rock
older than all my family's lifetimes
resting against the warm stone

seeing but not seeing
the beauty around me

the longer i sit
the more that's there
a grove of wildflowers to my left
where did they come from?
a tangled spider's web hung above in trees
did the spider just weave it?
a raven a few trees over
watching, for how long?

seeing but not seeing
the longer you sit in a space the more you will see

On Purpose
/ When Not Writing III

doubt
shackled to my mind
squeezing my internal organs
questions of real purpose

On Identity
/ Possession of Words/Owner of History/Belonging

what is my soul losing by not knowing cree?

On Grief
/ Always

the day
my mom called and told me they had found a mass on her lungs
i screamed into my pillow

my fingers hovered over the numbers to call you
but i couldn't press them
the moment i told you it would be real

you knew
when she passed,
in anger you had lashed out, and you knew
something was wrong
it was then that i told you

for months i had hidden my pain,
but then i couldn't hide it anymore

our cold hands clenched together as the light faded from the sky
i cried on the swing set and i tried to remember
the last words i said to my mom

you promised, always
we will always find each other
in the next place, we know where to meet
under a sign that reads 1056
i'll be on time,
you'll be late because you're never on time
but you always show up

On Teasing
/ Uncles

a whistle through teeth,
s s s s s s s s s s s

On Love
/ Planting

when you plant a seed
you don't see the whole of the tree right away
the fruit is not able to be harvested
until the year and season are right

i've planted seeds all over you

On Mental Illness
/ PTSD

i.

held down on a cold bathroom floor
the laughter of the girls
echoing off the tiled walls

fingers pushing themselves into me
as they violated every part of who i was
a game for them
a lifetime of trauma for me

after school
for weeks, months
taken from the playground
locked in the bathroom
with the girls, the fingers, the anything they could fit inside

all rape stories don't involve men
all rape stories don't involve adults
all rape stories don't look like what you think they look like

it wasn't enough for them to invade my body
they had to invade my mind also
mental torture
spinning in darkness

months of after school fear

ii.

laying on the operating table
invasion again
but this time to fix
the wounds from before
three times asleep
many more awake

cameras pushed inside
as the doctors
tried to heal
what couldn't be healed

iii.

pushed under rugs
trauma forces its way out over and over again
my parents choose to forget

i never had the option

symptom one: screaming when startled
symptom two: being easily startled
symptom three: nightmares
symptom four: making myself invisible
symptom five: not letting anyone love me
symptom six: never going into a public bathroom without fear
symptom seven: panic in a dark room, especially a bathroom
symptom eight: seeing a face in the tile, all tiles, always laughing at me
symptom nine: flashbacks at inconvenient times
symptom ten: knowing the worst can and will always happen

iv.

it's okay to feel anger when you've been raped

On Secrets
/ Things I Hate about Myself

that for so long i let my disorders take over my life and keep me trapped, literally, in my room and in my head

that i feel so much safer being alone that i've convinced myself i like being alone more than i like being with people

that excitement is a scary emotion for me because it can consume me

that i have to be afraid of happiness because the opposite of that is a deep depression and if i have one, i have to have the other one eventually

that i become obsessive about things to the point where i forget about anything else in my life but then just as quickly drop them and move on to something else, so everything in my life is just bursts of frantic energy

that i am sadness a lot of the time

On Secrets
/ Things I Love about Myself

that because of my obsessive tendencies i know random facts about so many things

that because of my self-inflicted secluded life i am really happy with who I am; i am comfortable with my own company for weeks, and i assume years, on end, i could totally last in a wasteland scenario with only myself as a companion

that because of my need to stay perfectly balanced in order to function, i am aware of my emotions at all times

that because i went through all the shit that i did i am a stronger, better person, someone that for a long time i didn't have the belief i would ever be able to become

that i can laugh through pain

On God
/ *Signposts*

i.

a moth the size of half my fist once crawled into my mouth while i was
asleep and died
i woke with it filling me
it happened during the darkest time in my life
when i was in the desert
not literally, of course
the metaphorical desert
like the one jesus went to
when he felt the farthest away from god that he ever had

that was me,
far away from god
and then a moth crawled into my mouth and died

ii.

signposts are events like déjà vu
or conversations meant to happen
moments that feel unreal but are tangible and right in front of you

signposts are messages from god,
or so i was raised to believe
they let you know you're on the right track
exactly where you're supposed to be

iii.

a moth crawled into my mouth and died
i thought it meant i was cursed
that i had abandoned god and that he had abandoned me
but a conversation over late nights
a throwing down of personal facts
lead me to share this story

a moth crawled into your mouth and died?

i know, gross right?

a moth crawled into your mouth and died???

i know, i have no idea why

a moth crawled into your mouth and died...

a contemplative statement

my throat became choked with tears
remembering how lost i was back then
how heart sick
how afraid

a moth crawled into your mouth and died

said with revelation

what are moths attracted to?

i dunno?

light

a moth crawled into my mouth and died
went i felt like i had no light inside of me
when i felt like i was only darkness
went i felt i had abandoned god and he had abandoned me

a moth crawled into my mouth and died
      because maybe even when i couldn't see it
i still had light inside of me

a signpost years later
because a moth crawled into my mouth and died

On Mental Illness
/ Ashes

i despise that i have to fear happiness, excitement
because at any moment
i can become too happy, too excited
and i can tip

the mania that smoulders inside of me
can flame at any moment
consume everything
leaving only grey and white ashes in its wake

On Identity
/ *Together*

and maybe that's the thing
everything that is me can't be put into separate boxes
i can't be spelled out in the blank space of a form
because i can't separate the loneliness from the hereditary pain,
from the abuse, from the soul-leeching coldness of having no emotion,
to feeling like life is a dream

it's all just me

On Grief
/ Being Okay Sometimes

only breaking down occasionally
burning plates of food for you at christmas
keeping your memory alive for your grandchildren who never got to meet you
living every day because
you would want me to

On Love
/ Harvest

grown like roots
our love tangles
through the rough underbrush of the forest
sending signals like how the trunks of fir trees
send water up through their branches

planted in smiles,
touches,
i-miss-you texts

from afar
the seed of love planted years before

waiting until now to harvest
all that we are

On Mental Illness
/ Living

i go about the business of living
just the way that i am
because what else can i do?

On Identity
/ Rooted

and so i guess i have claimed my mom's blood as my own
because it's from that blood that i have memory,
experience
even if i am
white passing

ACKNOWLEDGEMENTS

I want to thank all the Indigenous writers who have paved the way for me to have the courage to write this book.

I wrote this book for anyone who is struggling with their own issues surrounding their identity. It was a way to help me focus my thoughts and really look at who I am as a person and why I am as a person.

To any Indigenous youth out there who may be reading this: you matter, and these words are for you. I hope that if you're struggling, you'll do the same and try writing about all that you're feeling. Writing always helps. I have written my way out of more than one depressive episode and I'm sure I will again. Even if you don't think you're a writer, you are. Just try.

I need to give a special thanks to my sister Jennifer who always reads my work before anyone else. And to my sister Sabrina, who always encourages me to keep writing. To my grandma, who always, always, always believed in me and kept pushing me to finish my education and to live a good life. To my mom, who never got to see these poems, but who I know was sitting beside me as I wrote them. To my father, for loving me even when I didn't understand.

Thank you to all my friends who put up with my rambling, ranting and raving, who took the time to listen to me as I struggled to put thoughts into words, and for providing conversations that opened my mind and gave me my *aha* moments. You all have helped me far more than you know.

PREVIOUSLY PUBLISHED

"Build Up," "Packing," and "Through Ribs and Things" previously published by *The This Magazine*.

"Star Matter," previously published by *Red Rising Magazine*.

"Full Circle" and "Still, Beauty" previously published by *Hamilton Arts and Letters*.

"Origin of a Designation" and "Bannock," previously published by *Grain Magazine*.

ABOUT THE AUTHOR

Francine Cunningham is an award-winning Indigenous writer, artist and educator originally from Calgary, Alberta, but who currently resides in Vancouver, BC. Francine is a graduate of the Master of Fine Arts in Creative Writing program from the University of British Columbia, where she also graduated with a bachelor of arts in theatre.

www.francinecunningham.ca